Rope Your Dream

Make a dream come true
Improve yourself
Prepare for competition

By Monte Alkire

The Author and Publisher have no liability or responsibility to any person or entity with respect to loss or damage caused or alleged to be caused indirectly or directly by this book. Every effort has been made to avoid any errors or inaccuracies; nonetheless they may exist.

ISBN: 1-4196-9050-7

ISBN-13: 9781419690501

Library of Congress Control Number: 2008901464

Visit www.booksurge.com to order additional copies.

Dedication

To my wife Harriet for enduring encouragement, support and time sacrifice.

To the men and women of the United States Armed Forces who train, guard, and fight risking life and limb so we may be free.

Contents

Contents continued

Acknowledgements

Thank you for all the help.

Harriet Alkire my loving wife

Marc, Kim and Kathy our children,

Cliff and Betty Alkire, Dad and Mom

Ron Bachman, friend, roping partner, business partner, high school counselor

Tanner Bryson, friend, professional rodeo cowboy, roping instructor

Mary Einsel, friend, writer

Doyle Gellerman, friend, professional rodeo cowboy, roping instructor

Bobby Harris, friend, professional rodeo cowboy, roping instructor, my coach

Jim Hollister, friend, schoolteacher, writer, golfer

W. D. "Wally" Lowry, friend, Professor Emeritus, Virginia Tech

Walt Ward, friend, cowboy

Will Ward, friend, cowboy

Walt Woodard, professional rodeo cowboy, roping instructor

Acknowledgements

Thank you for the ideas and inspiration:

Ameircan Quarter Horse Association,
    America's Horse magazine

James E. Loehr, Ed.D.
    *Mental Toughness Training For Sports:
    Achieving Athletic Excellence*

Charles Pogue

Lance Armstrong (with Sally Jenkins)

Every Second Counts

Peoria Journal Star

Ralph Prideaux, R. D. Prideaux Photography

Pro Rodeo Sports News

Spin to Win Rodeo Magazine

SuperLooper Magazine and Walt Woodard

Tom Reilly, Tom Reilly Training

Courage in Sales

Tyler Magnus

United States Team Roping
    Championships, USTRC

Wrangler National Finals Rodeo

Foreword

If there are a few things that you would like to change for the better, this book may be able to help. It is not all invented here. This is a gathering of ideas and approaches that have worked well for others and myself. It spans input from my family, the factory floor of Caterpillar Inc., and the sports experiences of champions in everything from golf to bull riding, bicycling, tennis and sales. My lessons have come from people with backgrounds and skills as diverse as Lance Armstrong, Walt Woodard, and Tom Reilly.

The main impetus for gathering these ideas has been my own passion for team roping and the desire to use every resource available to try to improve. These are my thoughts and experiences collected over several years. The more I gather these ideas and approaches, the more I see their almost universal applicability.

This book has many references to team roping because that is my passion, but it's not about the technical aspects of team roping. It explains my approach to making a dream come true, improving performance and preparing for competition. It addresses mindsets and roadblocks on the journey toward excellence. The quotes are stories and experiences that helped me through various issues and serve as quick reminders to help me next time. This is the experience of a regular person who is stretching to realize a dream, and who didn't start until he was 54 years old.

Team roping has a lot in common with golf, tennis and baseball. All four sports require an instrument and a swing to succeed. The similarities are many. One major difference is the horse. The horse is the enabler in team roping.

The commitment statement, defining my "Right Attitudes Toward Excellence" stimulated significant improvement in my roping ability. In addition, it resulted in me collecting and organizing the information in this book.

While you pursue your passion, have this book readily available as a resource. Use it to refresh your mind during waiting time or down time. I like to review mine before competing in ropings and go over those things that have been giving me the greatest challenge recently. It is also nice to have a companion read them to you as you're driving or traveling, especially if he or she is your teammate. Eventually these concepts will be instilled in your thought process and behavior. Caution—it will take time, repetition and effort for these thoughts and behaviors to become automatic.

As you proceed, add your own findings, observations and great examples to this book. Your notes will personalize this resource and add value.

During the process of writing this book, I was interrupted during the winter of 2004-2005 and got away from these references. Looking back now, I am convinced that not having had these available to me, at my fingertips, if only for a casual reference, was a mistake. I missed the opportunity to use and review these during my winter roping season, resulting in a missed opportunity to avoid and respond to difficult situations. With this reference in hand, I am sure my performance would have been better. This experience gave me the motivation to continue the documentation work and not make the same mistake again.

As you read you might find yourself saying, "I know that" or "I have thought of that." The same thing happened to me as I tried to improve, but I found that if I didn't write the concept down and review it, I would forget it. That's why I wrote this book.

We need to be able to pull these concepts out quickly when we need them and continuously review them until they become habitual. I believe this book will help you excel in your endeavor. It will also serve as a basis of knowledge for you to build upon and personalize.

These thoughts and experiences are offered for improvement in your own endeavor, whether it is sport, business, or any personal goal. The material is organized by topic so you can start anywhere. I recommend you find the topic that is of the greatest interest at the moment and dive in. Good luck! Remember to have fun along the way.

Commitment Statement

If you're embarking on a new project, sport or job or have decided to take your performance to a new level, make a clear commitment statement to yourself. It should define where you are going and what you are committing to. My commitment statement follows:

Monte Alkire's Commitment To Excellence

I will always strive to give my best effort, regardless of the circumstances. I am never satisfied with giving less than 100 percent effort. I will always work to achieve the highest level of excellence I am capable of at the time. I have pride in what I represent and what I have accomplished as a team roper. Being true to myself and taking pride in what I do demands that I always give my best effort, no matter how badly the situation may have deteriorated. I'm not a quitter, and I'm willing to pay the price.

I've set goals for myself, and I'm willing to put forth whatever effort is necessary to accomplish them. If for any reason I should fail to

accomplish my goals, I will always know and take pride in the fact that I gave no less than my best. I fully understand that success is not waiting for something to happen, it's making it happen. I'm not content with simply holding my own. My attitude is offensive rather than defensive. I am active rather than reactive. I'm going for it!

Last but not least, I understand that my future as a team roper is in my own hands. What I accomplish and what I fail to accomplish is the result of me. I accept full responsibility for myself. My destiny is shaped and molded each day in accordance with what I dream, what I think and what I do. I will be successful!

— From *Mental Toughness Training For Sports: Achieving Athletic Excellence*, James E. Loehr, Ed.D., Page 72 and 73. Adapted and personalized by Monte Alkire, Aug. 12, 1998.

Thinking things through and getting your mind right when you start

Courage

*Courage: The ability to face
difficulty or danger with firm-
ness and without fear*

Courage is something most of us don't consider in our daily lives. We don't think about it as
we compete in sports, go to work, tackle a tough
assignment or deal with difficult family situations.
Most of us think of courage in terms of war situations or the brave acts of police officers, firemen,
and citizens in tough situations. I believe courage
enters our life far more than we realize. I hope this
will give you some cause to reflect on the subject
personally.

Let's relate courage to a sport. It takes courage
to compete in a sporting event. When I say compete, I mean going all-out to compete—putting
your money on the line and really trying to win!

Why does really competing take courage? Because competitors fear failure, loss of respect by
others, loss of money, loss of status, letting their
teammate down and, most important, the loss of
self-respect.

When I back into the box for a $100 prize at a
local roping event or for an $84,000 prize at the Na-
tional Championships, I want to win! If I don't win it
hurts—my pocketbook, yes, but mostly in my gut.
It takes courage to subject yourself to the possibility of failure.

Tom Reilly helped me take a new look at fear and the role of courage in everyday life. In his article, *Courage in Sales* Copyright 2003 (from his book *Value Added Selling*), Tom explained

I spent over four years in the US Army, from 1969–1973. As they prepared us for war, I remember well what they taught us about courage. Courage is not the absence of fear; it's the management of fear. I've thought about this a lot over the years, especially when confronted with experiences that required some courage to muddle through them. In fact, I've observed on more than one occasion that it's not courage if it doesn't involve fear. Some people have said about courage, "It's fear that said its prayers." Hemmingway wrote, "Courage is grace under pressure."

Courage is not limited to acts of bravery on a battlefield or struggling against the insurmountable odds of a fatal disease. We use courage to navigate much of life's tough experiences. We use courage in making the tough decisions of life. It takes courage to stand up to others when your principles tell you others are wrong. It takes courage to express creative ideas in the midst of "group-think."

Some days it takes courage just to get out of bed.

Successful sales people use courage for the tough situations in which they find themselves. For some, it takes courage to make cold calls, especially in an area filled with rejection. Some salespeople must rely on courage to make the tough calls and deliver tough news. Other salespeople use courage when they go to bat for the customer with their company or to go the bat for their company with their customer. And yet others use courage when they hold the line on prices. It takes courage to stand fast when the customer says, "Your price is too high!" First, customers test your price; then, they test your resolve. Courage is one of those things you can develop. It starts when you make a stand. You feel the fear and act in spite of the fear, not because of the fear. For salespeople, there is no success without courage.

President Theodore Roosevelt provided another perspective on courage:

It is not the critics who count, not the man that points out how the strong man stumbled or where the doer of deeds could have done better. The credit belongs to the man who is competing in the arena, whose face is marred with sweat, who strives valiantly, who errs and comes up short again and again, who knows the great enthusiasms, the great devotions, and spends himself in a worthy cause; who, at the best knows the triumph of achievement, and who at the worst, if he fails, at least fails while daring greatly, who knows that his place shall never be with those cold and timid souls who know neither victory nor defeat!

Walt Woodard speaks of courage in his monthly article in the April 2004 issue of the *SuperLooper Magazine*:

I listen to motivational speakers all the time on radio and TV, and they talk about all kinds of things that we need to do to become successful. The one thing they forget to mention is courage—without that, nothing great is possible. It takes courage to try to do things that not many before have done. You'll never know how you would have done unless you try. I have met people that won't compete unless all the conditions are in their favor. The only way they'll race is if you give them so much of a head start they know they will win and to that I say "chicken!" If they know they're the best they compete, but if they think the competition is a little too tough, they won't enter. This country wasn't built on that philosophy. Roll your sleeves up and get into the fight because anything might happen. I personally don't like to compete if I know I'm going to win. What would be the accomplishment in that? I want to try to slay a giant; try to do what other people think is impossible. People always talk about the fact that they hope someday their ship will come in—to that I say if you're tired of waiting, swim out to it. "Well what if I drown," they'll say. Well, at least you tried and you went down trying to accomplish something great and you didn't let fear hold you back.

Several years ago Lee Trevino was going to play in the Masters Golf Tournament, but a few days before he came down with pneumonia. He was very sick and he went to his doctor. After the visit his doctor suggested he should not play because he might get worse. Lee Trevino, always the optimist, had another thought; bet-

ter play—might even win. He played
and won second. Have the courage
to play with the bravery of a lion because you never know what might
happen.

Walt wrote the above in 2004. In 2007 he won
the USTRC National Championship and his second Professional Rodeo Cowboys Association
World Championship. Walt is over fifty years old.
That took courage and a lot of work. There are few
world championships won in rodeo or other sports
by competitors his age.

On October 12, 2007 I heard a caller on the
Rush Limbaugh Show explain how amazed he was
with Rush's ability to speak so effectively extem-
poraneously. He asked him, "How do you do it"?
Rush's first response was "through preparation
and knowledge of the subject." He explained he
uses no written monologues. Rush went on to say,
"I do it by passion, confidence and lack of fear."
This man has the most widely listened to radio talk
show in our country. He acknowledged the fear issue, which could be present in his work situation.
He has addressed and overcome the fear. Fear is
common.

In the spring of 2001, I went to the Scottsdale,
Arizona rodeo slack and Doyle Gellerman was
there. Doyle has helped me through his roping
schools and with personal encouragement over
the years. He asked me how my roping was going.
I responded that I was improving.

He said, "Oh, are you winning?"

I said, "Mostly, I'm practicing. I'm thinking about coming to your next roping school in Michigan." I had already been to three of his schools.

He said, "Monte, you don't need to go to more schools. You need to go out and compete."

Fear of losing or embarrassment held me back. Two years later I had won six saddles and numerous belt buckles and other prizes, to say nothing of the cash prizes. He was absolutely correct! I needed the *courage* to go out and compete!

In 1964 I went through U.S. Army Airborne Training at Fort Benning, Georgia. I volunteered. It was a tough three weeks and fear was a major factor. When the time came, would I really jump out of a perfectly good airplane? I did, five times, and what confidence and sense of accomplishment I gained from the experience! I still profit from those jumps today. The training was ten or eleven hours a day for three weeks, then we made our jumps. It was awesome, repetitive and strenuous until our actions were reflexive and our confidence incredible. During jump week we all performed wonderfully and earned the parachute badge. The bottom line is, we were prepared and confident, and we wanted the badge. The Army had prepared us well.

In our regular lives we are responsible to prepare ourselves. With preparation and a passion to succeed, we can muster the courage to succeed.

Sometimes you come face to face with the reality of a situation and ask yourself, "Have I got it in me?" Usually, if we have the passion, we do have it in us. If we really want it, we can do it.

Another thing—don't feel guilty or inferior because you feel fear. If fear wasn't common to many of us, there would not be so much written about courage.

Take Tom Reilly's advice: "Feel the fear and act in spite of it, not because of it. The rewards are incredible!"

Wishing, Willing and Working

Wish: 1. To feel an impulse toward attainment of something 2. To desire or yearn
Will: Used to express determination
Work: Exertion or effort directed to produce or accomplish something

These three things often get confused and entangled when people begin to accomplish something or raise their performance to a higher level. The following comments will help us recognize the difference and make the right choices.

So how do you go about excelling at your chosen activity? What does it take to best the competition and really be at the top end of your game? Too often, we humans look at those who are at the top of their game and marvel at their skills. We are prone to wish that we could do "that" or wonder at their talent. In all the cases I have seen and studied, the ability to excel is primarily the result of a strong will plus the dedication to perform the hard work necessary to achieve an extraordinary result.

Performance excellence is not a gift, it is not genetic alone, and it is not the result of environment. It is the result of dedication to accomplishing a goal. Some other examples follow.

There are two different kinds of people, those who wish and those who will. The wishers wish to be great at something or to be famous for some reason. The ones who will, they don't wish, they set a course and they do it. They become what they want to or get what they want.

Walt Woodard, World Champion Team Roper wrote the following in *SuperLooper Magazine* in Jan. 2001. It really helped me realize and think about the effort required to achieve a truly superior result. "I hear people say all the time, man, I wish I could do this or that and I always think the same thing. If they really wished it they could do it. I heard a story about Gary Player, the great South African golfer, during an interview with a reporter one time. The reporter said, 'I wish I could hit a golf ball like you.' Mr. Player replied, 'No you don't, because if you did, I mean truly did, you would hit golf balls until your hands broke open and bled, then tape your hands and continue.' He said he wasn't any more gifted than anyone else at birth. He knew what he wanted and he didn't mind the dedication. Most people don't want to hear that because it puts the pressure right back on us.

"Success is up to the individual. No one cares if we succeed or fail ... it is up to us. What is it that you want?"

Walt lives his philosophy. He won the World Championship with Doyle Gellerman in 1981. He won his second World Championship in 2007. We have few world champions, especially in rodeo, who are over fifty years old.

I went to Doyle Gellerman and Walt Woodard's team roping school in 1994. It was a life-altering experience for me. I started to really understand the difficulty of what was going to be required to learn to rope well.

Walt's brother Dale Woodard is also a professional team roper, rodeo clown and writer. I am privileged to know him as a friend, teacher and roping partner. He also enjoys a tremendous work ethic. I have heard him say on several occasions, "You have got to be willing to do what others won't, in order to have what others don't." —Dale Woodard, January 2002, Wickenburg, Arizona.

Lance Armstrong is one of my most respected athletes. He has accomplished what others thought impossible. He defines will and work by his example. In his book *Every Second Counts*, written with Sally Jenkins, he talks about turning points in his life. "There aren't many clearly marked, signpost moments in your life, but occasionally they come along, and you have a choice. You can either do something the same old way, or you can make a better decision. You have to be able to recognize the moment, and to act on it, at risk of saying later, 'That's when it all could have been different.' If you're willing to make a harder choice, you can redesign your life."

In 2004, Lance Armstrong won the Tour de France Bicycling Race for the sixth time. The *Peoria Journal Star* summed up his achievements in an editorial on 7-24-06: "Armstrong shows limitless power of will." They compared him to Mohammad

Ali, Tiger Woods, Jim Brown and Babe Ruth. I will add Ty Murray. Bernie Lincicome, of Scripps News Service, reported, "How few athletes had won 6 world titles in a row, even the Yankees haven't." The paper summed it up: "What a day, what a triumph, and what a valuable lesson for all of us in the limitless power of the human will." *Talk about will!*

Another example of Dale Woodard's work ethic comes thorough here.:"The will to win is useless without the willingness to prepare!" The willingness to prepare always translates into work. — Dale Woodard January 10, 2004, Wickenburg, Arizona.

These stories motivate me. It all comes down to what you want and how badly you want it. My approach to improvement in roping was developed with my partner, Ron Bachman, in 1994. We decided to become better than the average Illinois ropers. We knew that if we could do that, we would have a lot of fun and win some money in the process. We committed to more practice, greater study, and better practice to accomplish our goal. That kind of a goal is work. It is much more than wishing. We are making progress, but not without overcoming some obstacles. In addition to our roping, we have moved a barn, lost a house in a fire, each built a new house, suffered a few serious health issues and married off four of our children. In spite of these "noise factors" in our life, our roping is improving and we are really enjoying it.

Talent and Effort

Talent: A superior, inborn capacity for a special field
Effort: 1. Exertion of physical or mental power 2. A strenuous attempt

As we look at an athlete or anyone especially skilled at a certain task, often the first reaction is, *Wow, he/she really has a talent for that!* Often I was guilty of this "rush to explanation" as the reason for excellent performance or great skill.

In my school days I did not participate in the organized athletics regularly. I was small, slow maturing, and lived on a small farm. My family did not value sports proficiency. Work around home was praised and appreciated. So I grew up thinking there was a lot to this talent thing, never realizing the importance of effort. That changed in 1994, when I began to learn to rope in earnest. Oh how it changed!

When I started team roping the relationship between talent and effort became apparent. Yes, there is some latent talent in most of us, but it takes effort to bring it out, develop it and hone it to a fine skill. For some, it may come faster and easier; for others, more effort will be needed.

One starts to learn to rope by roping what we call a Roping Dummy, a small, simulated steer with horns and/or back legs to let us learn the mechanics and basic skills of "roping on the ground." This saves a lot of wear and tear on horses and cattle. It also drastically reduces the risk of injury to all three animal species (cattle, horses and humans). When I started throwing loops at the dummy, it sure seemed to come hard. My partner, Ron Bachman, was coaching and encouraging me. One night, while helping me overcome my frustration, he said, "It will probably take you 50,000 loops to develop a swing." That was pretty sobering to me because at that time I was throwing 10 loops a night when I did chores. You can do the math and see where that was headed… straight to nowhere.

Needless to say, I changed my approach to practice and over time enjoyed good results. I also defined my personal talent and effort equation. Ron underestimated the number of loops that all-important night. I believe it takes more like a million loops to develop proficiency and consistency.

Natural talent versus work is a subject often discussed in athletic circles. The following perspective by Walt Woodard helped motivate me: "So knowing that I wasn't blessed with natural talent, I decided I would out work people. Get there earlier, and stay later. Try hard and refuse to quit. When the struggle seems hopeless, tell yourself that your almost there. This must be the place that most people quit because the going is tough, but not me, I am not like most people… I don't quit. I don't get tired and I don't quit." — *SuperLooper Magazine*, April 2001.

Kirk Wessler wrote the following about professional female golfer Christie Kerr, on September 2, 2005 in the *Peoria Journal Star*. "Cristie is relentless, methodical, simultaneously fast and deliberate: a machine of practiced repetitive movement and ruthless efficiency." **I will work toward realizing this as a description of my roping.** This may fit into my goal statement.

Just in case you haven't come to grips with this yet on your own, here is how I sum it up:

Talent is God given!

Effort is a choice!

Talent + Effort = Results!

My recommendation: Put your whole heart into it!

Why?

Why: For what reason, cause or purpose

Why do you do what you do? You need a clear answer to that question. Without the clear answer, you might lack the punch to advance and excel.

In my case, why do I ride and rope?

Ever since I can remember starting to ride it seems that I always wanted to rope, but there were always obstacles. Early in life, it was the lack of friends who were doing this, a mentor, a teacher, a place, a horse, and time. Later it was the military and our growing family. Then finally in 1994 the resources and the time were available. I found my roping partner-to-be, Ron Bachman. He too was in need of a partner, and the opportunity was born.

When I can ride and rope I call it "living the dream," something I had dreamed about for years. Having always wanted it gives me the desire to advance and excel. That is my Why. It's Why I rope, Why I enjoy roping so much and Why I try to advance and excel. Plus, I must confess to just a teeny, tiny little competitiveness.

This question also brings to mind something I read while in college. How to be successful: "Find something you really like to do and get good at it." If you're asking yourself what to do, the above might help you find the answer.

Here are a few more perspectives from those who share a passion:

"Cancer made me want to do more than just live: It made me want to live in a certain way. The near-death experience stripped something away. Illness had left me with a clear view of the difference between real fear and mere disquiet, and of everything worth having, and doing.

"But some things in me won't change: I like to control things, like to win things, like to take things to the limit. A life spent defensively, worried, is to me a life wasted.

"So this (my book) is about life. Life after cancer. Life after kids. Life after victories. Life after some personal losses. It's about risk, it's about agenda, and it's about balance. It's about teeing the ball up high and hitting it hard while trying not to lose control. And if you shank it, then go and find your ball and try it again... because the way you live your life, the perspective you select is a choice you make every single day when you wake up. It's yours to decide." — Lance Armstrong (with Sally Jenkins) in *Every Second Counts*

Charmayne James is a supreme champion. I have admired her approach and results since she turned professional. Her sport is barrel racing. Here are some of her individual records:

First Million-Dollar Cowgirl, 1990

Most Consecutive Professional Championships, 11

Holder of More World Championships than any other woman in professional sports!

I heard her make this remark: "It is not about the money, the fame, or the prizes. It is about the satisfaction that comes from hard work, commitment, and focus resulting in success." She summarizes the "why" with one word: **satisfaction**.

I can tell you for certain; the only reason I work on roping is for my personal satisfaction. Sure it feels like work some days, but the thought about what it will eventually yield gets my blood pumping.

Maybe you think you're too old or too whatever to get excited about something. Frankly, I don't buy that. I just love this quote from 68 years old Boots O'Neal, the Four Sixes Ranch, in *America's Horse* magazine: "I caught a horse before daylight every day last week, and while I was saddling I was still excited about what we were going to do that day."

What a great outlook on life.

Passion

Passion: An intense, extreme or overpowering emotion

Usually the reason behind the "Why" is passion. My passion is roping and, of course, that involves horses.

I love horses and I wanted to cowboy, ride and rope for as long as I can remember. Every day I can ride, I consider a gift from God. The days I am able to rope are very special gifts. And the days when I am able to ride and rope, when my horse works especially well, or when I am roping better than usual are special, blessed gifts. On the days when we can win in competition, it is difficult to find the words to be properly thankful to God.

When I was working at Caterpillar, Caterpillar was my passion. I devoted all the hours available to Caterpillar on a daily basis for years. There are a lot of us who share the passion. They say those of us in the Caterpillar family have yellow blood. It is a great company, a great product, a great dealer organization and a great place to work.

Naturally, the pursuit of my passion is secondary to the happiness and well being of my family and friends.

If you are really going to excel, you must have the passion.

Horses

Horse: A wonderful four-legged animal (my personal definition)

It is difficult for me to discuss passion without thinking of horses. To me, horses are wonderful. There is an old saying: "There is something about the outside of a horse that is good for the inside of a man." I am living proof of that. I doubt that I would have survived the pressure of my last 20 years at Caterpillar without my horses for stress relief. We all need something to escape to, relax with, and help clear our mind and body of tension. My something is the horse. If you look at how I spend my time in retirement it is evident that I enjoy the time I spend with my horses more than the time I spend with most people I know. On many days my only social contact is with my horse.

At the present time I ride horseback about 700 hours per year. On September 19th, 2007, I achieved 5,000 hours riding horseback over the last twelve years. That is the top recognition level for "time riding" given by the American Quarter Horse Association, and it's another indication of how much I enjoy horses. The summer of 2007 has been especially great as I have been training horses and practicing roping with a neighbor, Joe Bachman, four or five hours a day. We have learned a lot from each other and made excellent progress with our horses.

In team roping the horse is the enabler. Think about a batter and his stance, a golfer and his stance, a tennis player moving into position for contact with the ball. In roping, all the positioning and timing is provided by a horse. Communication and teamwork with the horse is essential to success. You must communicate through your body to your horse where you want to be at 30 miles per hour. Plus, you are pursuing a moving target that is trying to escape. Usually this all takes place in six to eight seconds. Consider the advantage I have over ropers who don't really love horses. The passion and enjoyment all come together for me in team roping.

When you are team roping you are always training, fine-tuning and developing your horse, not only basic roping and performance skills, but also training each other as a team. And I do mean training each other. You must learn to communicate very well to optimize each other's skills.

I've said for years that finding a horse to suit you, one you really like, is the next toughest thing to finding a wife. No joke here. I read the other day that Roy Rogers said almost the same thing years ago. He was one of my role models too.

Champion

Champion: A person who has defeated all opponents in a competition and thus holds first place

You will find that I will often quote champions. They have excelled; they are the best; they topped their game. Personally I have been blessed with many championships. It is important that we reflect upon and understand what a champion really is.

A champion is a winner. Champions excel and exceed their personal best, and thus they are champions. Of course there cannot be a champion without competition. Many of us thrive on competition. That is what makes the championship so sought after and desired. Competition helps define and reveal your true character.

Adversity

Adversity: 1. An unfortunate event 2. An event that opposes one's interests

Naturally when anyone sets out to accomplish something difficult there are always obstacles. The key to addressing obstacles is to realize they will be there, so prepare to react when they occur and do not let them get you down or get the best of you. Another approach is to somehow turn an obstacle into an advantage. This might seem like a "Pollyanna" concept in some respects, but you might be surprised how often it is possible when you approach the situation with this possibility in mind. The situation below is an outstanding example.

I remember watching a bull riding event in which the rider had drawn a really rank bull. One announcer was being very sympathetic to the bull rider and elaborating about how difficult the ride would be. The other commentator explained this could be a perfect draw, because it would keep him from being complacent.

At first, the remark seemed laughable but on second thought, what a great reaction. When the rider came out on that bull, he certainly wasn't complacent. He was bucked off, but not due to complacency.

When adverse situations arise, remind yourself to stay flexible. Flexibility, reactive instinct, alertness, and calling upon all your training when you need it—these traits will enable you to overcome obstacles and the competition.

Approach and Game Plan

Approach: A means of attaining a goal
Game Plan: A method of doing or proceeding to achieve victory beforehand

Whether it is preparing for a presentation on the latest and greatest something-or-other or getting ready for the next roping, sometimes we don't plan. We can become too focused on the topic or task. We can become so engrossed with mechanics, the thrill of being there, and the excitement of going that we forget to factor in all the important variables. In roping it's the arena, the box, the cattle, the score, your partner, etc. We must properly prepare ourselves for what might happen, what will most likely happen, and how to respond in either case.

In the early 2000's Champion Professional Team Roper Tanner Bryson was helping me with my roping and I was picking his brain on how I could do a better job in competition. He had seen me rope and knew I could catch steers. The first thing he said was, "Have a game plan and follow it. When something happens, change it on the fly if necessary." I know that seems pretty basic, but in all honesty, how often do you go out for that day of competition or to the big meeting and find yourself fully prepared as described above?

Here is how Charmayne James put it as she was preparing to enter the Wrangler National Finals Rodeo to try to win her 11th World Championship in Barrel Racing. "I knew Cruiser (her horse) had it in him and I just wasn't giving up. I was going to try as hard as I could and keep everything together, not get too excited, not get too up or down, just stay focused on what is important". – Pro Rodeo Sports News

The next time you head out for an event, large or small, be sure you have a game plan and alternate approaches in case something changes. I will wager you will enjoy the event much more and achieve better than average results.

Goals

Goal: An end that one strives to attain

More books have been written on goals than I can count. I do want to state that I am a firm believer in them and worked with them routinely for over 30 years in my jobs at Caterpillar. There, they were often called *objectives*.

Setting goals is really tough for me. To get a clear description of what I am really after and to make it reasonable, attainable, and still a stretch is a whale of a challenge. I really struggle with it, but it is worth the struggle.

One of the most lasting and memorable goals I can remember outside my family goals came from Walt Dunbar, my plant manager at Caterpillar in Davenport, Iowa. In 1981 Caterpillar was under duress due to the world economy, the Russian trade embargo, a weak dollar, and our own inefficiencies. The Davenport plant was trying to grow and overcome a jaded reputation for quality and efficiency. Walt gave us the goals of 1-100-1,000: 1% or less production lost to scrap or rework; produce parts and tractors to 100% of the production performance standard; and design and build tractors that would run 1,000 hours without a repair. They seemed unattainable. We achieved the first two in a year or so and made good progress on the

1,000-hour goal. Twenty-six years later I still remember this goal. Walt was one of the finest
leaders I ever worked for, including my military experience. Other bosses who were excellent with
goals were Curt Koch, Jean Claude Bonnevie, Jim
Despain, and our CEO in the 90's, Don Fites.

Walt was also unique with his explanation as to
why these goals were so lofty and tough. I can still
hear him say, "I know you can do it. It wouldn't be
fair if I didn't ask you to!" Now how can anyone say
no to a challenge set in that perspective?

Work at setting your goals. Use any help and
resources available; friends and partners can be
invaluable. Be tough with yourself, but realistic. It
may take some time to define what you are really
after.

Walt Woodard's approach has really helped me
pick my goals. Here is his approach:

1. Be specific. Pick out something, anything,
   and go after it! We must be realistic, but there
   are a million things within our reach!
2. We have to have our goal in our mind, exactly what we want and a time limit for earning
   it. Write it down and start working to attain
   or achieve it. Think about your goal the first
   thing in the morning, the last thing at night,
   and as many times during the day as possible.
3. Make it your desire; get it in your subcon-
   scious mind and make it happen.
4. If you want it badly enough, you will get it.

5. What the mind of man can conceive and believe, he can achieve!"
   > —Super Looper Magazine, *Jan 2001*

When you choose your goals, you need a clear understanding of whether you are going to try to jump over a picket fence, a clothesline or a windmill.

Focus

Focus: 1. Any center of activity or attention 2. The ability to ignore large distractions and to concentrate on the process

Focus takes training, practice, and tremendous resolve. Shutting out intervening thoughts and outside influences is difficult and truly an acquired skill. I have read everything I could get my hands on about this subject and practice it at every opportunity. I use numerous day-to-day situations to help me learn about and practice focus, which I truly believe is the key to success and victory. Below are a couple of examples that have helped me.

The Tour de France is a true sports spectacle and one of the most demanding of all sporting events. Think about it—how many other events require 23 days of peak performance in close succession? For that reason and others, I have long admired Lance Armstrong. The following are a couple of excerpts from his book on focus. "If you want to do something great, you need a strong will and attention to detail. If you surveyed all the greatly successful people in this world, some would be charismatic, some would be not so; some would be tall, some would be short; some would be fat, some would be thin. But the common denominator is that they're all capable of sustained, focused attention." — Lance Armstrong (with Sally Jenkins) in *Every Second Counts.*

If you think focus or concentration is a light matter, it is not. Consider this comment by Albert Einstein: "Even when tying my shoes, I am focused primarily on tying my shoes."

Test yourself. How good are you at focus? We can't expect to accomplish something very challenging without the same sort of focus. We can't succeed without it.

On so many occasions I have not been focused. When we set out to realize our dreams, we must prepare to focus. Work at it; the rewards will be fantastic.

Persistence

Persistence: Continuing, especially in the face of opposition

Persistence is a hallmark trait of successful people. When I get frustrated and begin to wonder whether I am making progress or ever will, it helps me to reflect on some very successful people whom I really admire. Many believe you only fail when you stop trying. It is easy to let yourself give up, but the great ones never do. They just keep trying. So often at our ropings someone will make a mistake, or a partner will miss and the roper will just give up. You can see this in all kinds of sporting events over and over. Some refer to it as *momentum*. The great ones overcome negative momentum. One of my personal heroes is Billy Etbauer. He is arguably the greatest bronc rider of all time and one of the most humble and sincere individuals you will ever hear interviewed. On top of that, he just doesn't know the meaning of giving up, and that's what makes him such a great champion. He has won five National Championships riding saddle broncs. In 2005 at age 41 he won or tied 5 of the 10 go-arounds at the Wrangler National Finals Rodeo, earning over $120,000 in winnings in 10 days. He has won over $1,000,000 in total at the Wrangler National Finals Rodeos in Las Vegas. There is much to learn from his attitude.

The following example of persistence was awesome and gut wrenching to watch. Put yourself in gymnast Paul Hamm's place and try to imagine his personal persistence and ability to focus on the next event.

"America's Golden Gymnast Teaches a Life Lesson"

"One of the great things about the Qlympics is the life lessons it teaches: The value of hard work; Making your best effort at all times; The importance of being a gracious winner and an honorable loser; never giving up.

"Gymnast Paul Hamm demonstrated many of those Wednesday, especially the latter. It took him to a gold medal in the all-around competition, America's first gold in that Olympic competition.

"The 21-year old Waukesha, Wisconsin native was one of the favorites at the Athens Games. But on his fourth exercise, the vault, Hamm had a gymnastics disaster. He fell, and what a fall. Awkwardly he fell off the mat nearly into the judges' table where they were scoring the event. Hamm dropped to 12th place. In a sport where tenths and hundredths of a point usually determine winners and losers, Hamm appeared to have lost his chance for a medal.

"On the sidelines, Hamm was stoic. He didn't hang his head or look beaten. Just focused on his last two exercises. A good routine on the parallel bars raised him to fourth, still off the medal stand. In the made-for-television drama that unfolded,

Hamm was the last competitor of the night...this time on the high bar, his best event. He was superb, three times flying off the bar and catching it, before sticking the landing. When his nearly perfect score was posted, Hamm had won the gold medal by .012, the closest margin in Olympic history." — *Peoria Journal Star*, editorial, 8-20-04

Paul Hamm proved the value of never giving up. Just imagine the focus and persistence required to overcome such a setback. Paul Hamm will always stand out as a remarkable champion.

Read the book *Endurance* by Alfred Lansing if you ever think you can't do something. It is the story of Sir Ernest Shackleton and 27 men fighting to survive a shipwreck in Antarctica. It will give you new vigor for anything you attempt. Those who excel, persist.

Success

Success: A favorable result

Success is up to the individual. No one cares whether we succeed or fail; it's up to us. Success can also be a very misleading state that we aspire to achieve. Before we start working toward success we need to take time to consider what will define a successful outcome of our effort.

Each individual defines success for himself or herself. Don't let others influence your opinion of your success. You know what you want, you set the goal, and you assess the results. That is what is important. Not everyone desires to be a world champion. Make sure you achieve what is important to you. When you are working toward a goal, I find that keeping a record of "personal bests" is a great way to acknowledge progress and create self-assurance that you are indeed improving.

Walt Woodard reminds us that success is elusive and often difficult to achieve, but we should enjoy the journey toward it. "People constantly tell me they are really getting frustrated and that always stuns me. My God, you just started. Nothing great was ever achieved without a struggle and the greater the struggle the sweeter the reward. People want immediate results and I believe patience is a virtue. Success is measured in inches and you need to just keep doing what you're doing. Stay positive and be persistent and the success you desire will come. You have to remember that it won't come

overnight. If it did everyone would be successful."
— Walt Woodard, *SuperLooper Magazine*, November 2002.

One way to help enjoy the journey is to dress for success. Personally I know that I do better in competitions when I am dressed smartly, have my horse groomed and my tack clean and in perfect shape. It seems to uplift my whole attitude, my self-confidence and my desire to excel. Being totally prepared adds to my confidence and feeds my fire of flaming enthusiasm. Flaming enthusiasm can be difficult for your competitors to overcome. If it works for you, do it!

Success is whatever you want it to be. Tie it in with your goals. Take things a step at a time. Celebrate small victories. Use your data and be certain every personal best is noteworthy. That is how to enjoy the journey. That is how you can rope your dream.

Monte, (on right), heading a steer for Sergio Mirales at
Cactus Country, Aguila, Arizona 2008 Photo courtesey
R. D. Prideaux Photography

Monte (on right) turning a steer for Buck Tuttle, Cactus Country,
Aguila, Arizona 2008
Photo courtesey R. D. Prideaux Photography

Dealing With Issues That Arise Along The Way

Accountability

Accountability: Liable to be called to account; responsible

If you approach your endeavor with the clear understanding that you alone are responsible for what happens, it will be a lot simpler when you respond to the results.

My wife, Harriet, summed it up this way: "If it is to be, it is up to me!" Having said that doesn't leave much room for doubt. When things go well, look in the mirror and be grateful for the success. With less than desired results, be prepared to accept responsibility and take action.

Or, as Ty Murray said: "When you win it is your fault! When you lose it is your fault!" – Pro Rodeo Sports News.

This is a bare-bones approach to accountability. Just think what a different world it would be in business, politics, sports and your personal life if everyone took this approach. There is no place to start like home and no time like the present.

Advice

Advice: Opinion given as to what to do; counsel

Whatever you set out to do there will always be people around you with lots of advice. On days when you are struggling, you will find yourself surrounded by people just waiting to function as advisors. I have found that most of them know less about what is happening than you do. You have to learn when to listen and when to tune it out. One thing to remember, a person doesn't necessarily know anything just because they have an opinion.

It is important that you can recognize who really knows and who just thinks that they know. Here is another reason I value professional help.

Apologies

Apologize: To express regret for a fault or mistake

Apologies are often considered a sign of weakness. I apologize for a lot of mistakes, but not when I miss in roping. I will be polite and let my partner know I was doing my best. If you're doing your best, there is nothing to apologize for. When you agree to rope with someone, you accept the risks that go with the sport. One of those risks is human fallibility, and that makes errors possible.

This is a situation that I will never forget. When beginners start competitive roping it is hard to get partners. It costs money to enter and you don't win if you don't catch; nonetheless, somehow you have to learn to rope in competition with the pressure of winning or losing. When I started roping, Herb Snow would always rope with me even though he knew our chances of winning were minimal. At one of my first competitions I missed my steer for Herb. I rode back to him and said, "Herb, I'm sure sorry."

He looked at me, disgusted, and said, "Sorry? Were you trying?"

I said, "I was trying as hard as I could." Herb said, "That's all that I ask and expect, so if you're trying, don't ever tell me your sorry again!"

I really respect Herb. I have never forgotten that and I have tried to never say that to a partner since.

I will say something, but I won't say I'm sorry—not when I'm trying—and I always try. If you're trying to do your best there is nothing to apologize for. In 2003, Herb and I qualified for the USTRC National Finals in Oklahoma City, Oklahoma and placed in the top twenty.

Blame

Blame: To accuse of being at fault

I will not blame others. It is a waste of time.

My point is, accept the accountability for failure as well as success. When I don't win or succeed, I ask myself what I could have done to avoid or prevent the problem. Almost always, there is something that I could have done to improve the situation.

Caution Versus Ferocity

Caution: To do something with great care to avoid injury or misfortune
Ferocity: The state of being extremely fierce and very intense

The approach to an event or situation is always important when preparing a game plan and executing it. The degree of caution or aggressiveness is important. I find the choice between caution and aggressiveness a delicate balance. It is easy to err both ways. In roping, when one is too cautious, we often use the expression "I safed-up." My experience is that I have lost more ropings to "safing-up" than I have to being too aggressive or ferocious. That's my personal history. For the last year or more, I have reminded myself before every run to be aggressive. For the coming year, I will remind myself to be ferocious. I expect this to be instrumental in taking my roping runs to a higher level.

One question that has helped me is, *Why take second place when first is available?*

Continuous Improvement

*Continuous: Going on with-
out interruption
Improvement: Improved over
a previous condition*

When I started roping, I believed, "I will learn to rope; then, I will have it." This is naïve because many around us are continuously improving. There are new competitors, younger competitors and new techniques. The bar is constantly being raised.

It is all about improvement. If your not going forward, you're falling behind. It is like Janet Huser told my wife and I one day as we were visiting their farm and the washing machine was running. It was kind of a wet, muddy day and they have four girls. I made a remark about her having a lot of laundry. She said, "You're darn right. If I am awake and that machine isn't running, I'm falling behind."

You're probably wondering what Janet's situation has to do with improvement. Whatever you're engaged in, trying to excel is much like Janet keeping up with her laundry. Every hour of every day there are people out there working to get better. So like Janet's washing machine, when you're awake you need to be running, going hard to stay ahead.

I remember a story about business competitiveness. It compared business to animal life in Africa, and it went something like this. When the sun comes up in Africa, you'd better be ready to run.

When the lion wakes up he stretches. He feels the hunger in his belly. He sees his cubs playing and knows they are hungry. He knows that if they will eat today, he must outrun the slowest gazelle in the herd nearby. When the gazelle wakes up he too stretches in the warm sun. He flexes his legs. He knows that to survive he must outrun the fastest lion in the brush.

It is like that in sports and in business too. If you want to excel, you had better be working harder, faster and better than your competition.

Billy Etbauer is one of my most admired athletes. He is the epitome of extraordinary success and a humble attitude. When interviewed after winning round eight of the Wrangler National Finals Rodeo on December 12, 2003 he said, "I don't think I ever got off a horse when I didn't know that I could have ridden him better." That is the attitude that creates a legend.

Trevor Brazile reached $1,000,000 in earnings faster than any other timed-event cowboy in rodeo history. His comment—"I think if you're ever content, you need to quit." – Pro Rodeo Sports News. He has gone on to win the World Championship All Around Cowboy title four times. In 2007 he won three World Championships in one season. He is only the third cowboy to ever achieve this success.

These people help kindle my fire to improve. They are role models for success through continuous improvement.

Ask that person who watches you shave or put on makeup every morning, "How can I do better?"

Data

Data: Facts or figures from which conclusions can be drawn

As you start working on your passion and striving for continuous improvement, the question will eventually come up: "How am I doing?" Keep records and use them as a motivator to chart your improvement and reward yourself for your accomplishments. What gets measured gets done. If you have sound goals, develop a metric to monitor your progress. Records will enhance and accelerate your journey to success. If you're not keeping score, it is only practice. I keep score in practice too, because I know it helps me. I can better see incremental improvement, and that motivates me. My partner, Ron Bachman, is a very intuitive and perceptive person. He does not rely on data like I do, but I have often seen him use it. He also uses a lot of data on the track team he coaches.

I have developed metrics for all facets of my roping activity. Roping the dummy standing on the ground, catches, types of catches, time for runs, number of barriers, short-round performance, total runs each day by horse used, and more. It is a long list. I even use statistical process control to monitor the trends. Bobby Harris enjoys teasing me about my statistics; nonetheless, they work for me.

If you work for a company or run your own business, think of the various critical activities or results that get measured. Every professional sport has several important statistics. Watch or listen to any business or sports broadcast and notice all the statistics reported. Professional wage contracts are heavily influenced by the individual's personal stats. It works for them. Why not use this tool to succeed in your passion?

Distractions

Distractions: Anything that draws the mind in another direction

Whether in business or sports situations there are always distractions. These distractions will eat you alive, given the opportunity. For example, at a roping all the players are there in the waiting area or off to the side in the arena and most of them are talking. They are buying or selling horses, discussing the weather, running down or picking apart the cattle, or picking out the best looking cowgirls or cowboys. When I am at a roping, I am there to rope and I am roping to win. You absolutely must be prepared to deal with distractions.

Dale Woodard told me this story about Jimmie Cooper's approach to dealing with distractions: "When I approach the area around the box, I liken it to a swimming pool. I think of myself as diving into the deep end and going to the bottom and staying until I start my run. This analogy helps me insulate myself from all the sights and sounds around me while in the box, much as if I were underwater." — Jimmie Cooper, repeated by Dale Woodard, 1-12-03.

This analogy is really important for ropers. There are always a bunch of competitors gathered tight around the box just talking or giving free, unsolicited advice. Sometimes it is done seriously with the intention of helping, sometimes they are just giving you the raspberry, and other times it is done maliciously to give you bad information on a steer or the score line. You must be able to blank it out.

If you think your situation is tough as far as distractions, think about the Tour de France. This is a 23-day race going six to eight hours a day with a swarm of competitors all around you, and the race is lined almost every inch with fans. Imagine the tempting distractions. Use this reference to develop techniques to deal with your distractions.

Excuses

Excuse: A cause, factor, or circumstance that frees one from blame

Excuses for poor results are of no value in making progress. Reasons help one understand, change and improve.

"Excuses are the tools of the incompetent.

Upon which monuments of nothingness are built.

Those who specialize in them, specialize in nothing else." — Anonymous, Provided by Marc Alkire, 2-5-04

Herb Snow and I were discussing competing with younger people and additional challenges we face. Herb and I are both eligible for Social Security. I didn't start roping seriously until I was 54, and Herb and I are the same age. We absolutely will not let age be an excuse for poor results. We also do not avoid competition with the young ropers. We never use our age as an excuse for a substandard performance or as a reason not to enter a roping event. Herb passed this along one morning: "Age and cunning can overcome youth and enthusiasm." I just love his reasoning. Along with age comes a very valuable dose of experience.

The next time something goes wrong, don't make excuses. Instead, look for the reasons and determine what you can do to fix it.

First or Losing

First: Being before all others with respect to time, rank, and order—important
Losing: To fail to have or get, to fail to win, to surrender or relinquish

"You can't go out there and try not to lose. You have to go out and try your best to win.... every time. I never went to a rodeo to finish fourth. I wanted to be first. I'd rather lose trying to win, than lose by sitting back and letting those other guys win." — Ty Murray, August 2000, *Pro Rodeo Sports News.*

This outlook is profound and now, thanks to Ty, imbedded in my mind as it has become second nature. It took me a long time to totally internalize it, probably due to the fear of failure of going all out, which usually involves taking more risk. But often, even when you go all out it is hard to win because so many others are going all out too. Give it all you have and what will be will be.

When I try not to lose I safe-up and almost inevitably make a mistake. We must stay aggressive, be ferocious, and go for a win.

Strive to be all that you can. Don't settle for second when first is available. Strive to be so good that you are awarded no handicap.

Mental Toughness

Mental Toughness: A mind that is firm, resilient and has great endurance

This might be the most critical trait to extreme success in your endeavor. Some say it is 80% to 90% of realizing peak performance. Mental toughness is all about staying focused, avoiding anger, fear and other counterproductive emotions, and calling up your peak-performance capabilities when you need them.

There are many aspects to mental toughness and there are some great books written on this subject. This was an area that I found sorely in need of strengthening and understanding. When I started roping it became quite clear I needed major improvement. Mental toughness is a critical skill. It takes work, but the results are very rewarding.

In roping you can't afford to miss. You miss and you're out. One bad loop, one poor start with your horse, one bad handle for your heeler and it is over. That creates pressure, and the more money that's on the line, the more pressure it creates. At most events we pay $20 or $25 per roper to enter one time. Normally 2/3 of this goes into the jackpot and 1/3 to the producer for cattle and labor. First-place checks of $300 to $800 for each roper are common. That gets my attention. The highest entry fees I ever paid were $350 per roper and I entered twice. It was a good investment. I won a saddle, a buckle and about $2,700 that day at the Jackrail Ranch in Aguila, Arizona. The most money I ever roped for was a first-place prize of $84,300 in the USTRC at Oklahoma City. That kind of an event will get your attention and test your mental toughness. My partner, Herb Snow, and I placed in that one also, finishing in the top twenty in the #6 USTRC National Championship in 2003.

You have to think about getting your mind right. Don't assume that it will happen automatically. My personal commitment statement is a good booster for me.

Sometimes in a tough spot you can try too hard and psyche yourself out of a good run. This is ridiculous when you really know how to do it and have done it hundreds or thousands of times. Somehow you need to avoid over thinking and still be cognizant of the situation. You've got to learn how to free your mind to direct your body.

Charles Pogue is one of my true heroes as a roper. He has qualified for the Wrangler National Finals Rodeo several times and won the aggregate there for roping the most steers in the least time in ten rounds. He is an outstanding horseman, a true gentleman and a cowboy role model. He commented on mental fatigue: "Mental fatigue is a big obstacle for all of us. We get tired. You can't concentrate all day long when you have two hours between runs. It's impossible. So you've got to be able to turn it off and go relax... a while; then turn it back on when it's time to rope again." — Charles

Pogue, *Spin to Win Rodeo Magazine*, September 2003.

Tyler Magnus was commenting on peers in the November 2002 *Spin To Win Rodeo Magazine* "Tee Woolman is the greatest horn roper I've ever seen as far as roping cow horns with finesse and grace, and he's a winner. Joe Beaver and Tee have similar personalities. They are the biggest bear in the woods, even if they haven't caught one in a month of Sundays. That's what it takes to be great for a long time." I really liked that part about "biggest bear in the woods," even when you aren't "on your game" so to speak. That takes mental toughness.

Bobby Harris is another example of supreme confidence. I have never heard him say it, but you can't be around him long without thinking, *This is the biggest bear in the woods.* He believes he can do anything with a rope and has often proved the point.

Even with all this good background and theory it doesn't always work. I like Ty Murray's classic cowboy logic: "Sometimes you get in a tough spot, make a tough draw. When you do all you can do, that's all you can do." — *Wrangler National Finals Rodeo Commentary.*

There at least two outstanding books on this subject: *Mental Toughness Training for Sports: Achieving Athletic Excellence,* by Ed J. Loehr and *The Inner Game of Tennis* by W. Timothy Gallwey. These are must-reads.

Mistakes

Mistake: An idea, answer or act that is wrong; an error or blunder

Roping is like most sports, intolerant of mistakes. Most business situations are the same way. But if we are doing things, we are going to make mistakes; that is human nature. In my first job as a test engineer at Caterpillar I was very upset and intolerant of myself when I made a mistake on some calculation or project decision. It really bothered me because I knew it was a waste of money.

Every spring Caterpillar had a management meeting for all the management employees in the Peoria, Illinois area. In the spring of 1969 I went to the meeting and our Vice Chairman of the Board Bill Nauman was the featured speaker. Bill was what we called a hard-way guy. He started out running a machine tool in our shop and worked his way to the top. At that meeting he talked about making mistakes: "I know that we all make mistakes, and when we do we feel bad about it. I make mistakes too. My mistakes cost the company a lot more money than yours do." This has stuck with me for these 38 years. His remark helped me so much then, and it has ever since. It serves me well in my roping today. One must acknowledge that mistakes will happen.

So how must we react?

Mistakes are hard on focus, self-confidence and self-esteem. Therefore the more skilled we become at dealing with them, the easier it becomes to excel over the competition. Mistakes present an outstanding opportunity to learn. Evaluate what happened, make a judgment on the cause and implement a corrective action. The process is the same in engineering, marketing, manufacturing or sports. In production circles it is often referred to as PDCA, Plan, Do. Check, and Act. It is the same basic process. If you have time between actions you can take some time to use this process or even consult others. In a rapid-fire situation like tennis, you must turn this over to the mind and body and let them react together.

It pays to have a short memory. You must evaluate a mistake, make a correction and move on to executing the improvement. Time spent commiserating over past mistakes reduces your ability to focus on the next event and will add to the problem. Here again, make an improvement and be positive about the next outcome.

Almost all mistakes are not earthshaking or life altering. They're only minor blips on our path to excellence. If you should make a mistake, there will always be another day. Focus on the future and plan for success.

Mistakes of others may upset you and interfere with your own performance. Here is a situation that helped me learn to get on with it. In 1984, I was Quality Manager at the Caterpillar Davenport, Iowa plant. We produced parts for Cat equipment and assembled track-type loaders. We were working hard to produce products with superior quality. Caterpillar corporate had outsourced many parts to Europe and Japan due to the currency exchange rates. In too many cases, incoming parts quality was unacceptable. It was my job to fix the problems, working with our purchasing department and other Caterpillar plants.

One particularly tough morning, the assembly line was almost shut down due to parts quality. I was on the line when my boss, Walt Dunbar, the plant manager, came along to see how things were going. I updated him on what we were doing. Then I made the mistake of telling him, again, the mistake the corporate office had made in outsourcing the parts. I can still feel and hear his response. He came within about twelve inches of my face, took his index finger and thumped me repeatedly on my breastbone. "You're whistling up a dead horse's butt. The quicker you get these problems fixed the better off we will all be." I got the message. I was on a plane to Europe shortly thereafter, and sure enough, things did get better. It always tickled me that Walt put that lesson in language he knew I would understand.

A team roper also has to deal with the mistakes he makes with his horse. You teach them wrong, lose your temper with them and often fail to see a situation through the horse's eyes. One day after such a mistake, Walt Ward said to me, "One thing about horses, Monte—they are very forgiving." He has been proven correct several times since.

When mistakes happen, stay positive, examine your own performance, review the basics, and strive to improve. Mistakes present a fantastic opportunity to improve!

Perfection

Perfection: a person or thing that is the perfect embodiment of something

Perfection is often desired but very difficult to realize. We look at the athletes who top their sports and we see them as perfect. In reality, they are chasing perfection like the rest of us; they are just closer to it than we are. Also, what is perfect for one professional might not be for another. One day at the Bobby Harris Roping Camp, we were working on our roping swings and were all trying to emulate Bobby. Bobby has a great, fluid swing and of course none of us could match it. He said, "You don't have to have a perfect swing to be successful, but you must understand the fundamentals to place your rope." Bobby's comment helped me a lot. It gave me a lot of confidence in my own swing and motivated me to keep trying to improve.

Positive Attitude

*Positive: Having a
constructive mindset
Attitude: A manner showing
one's feelings or thoughts*

Attitude is a huge factor in achieving success. I use it to my advantage in everything I do, especially my roping. Many times people have said to me after we have made a run and are discussing it on the way back up to the arena, "I just love to rope with you! You have such a great attitude!" Those remarks help us both to do even better next time.

I hate to be around negative people and I strive to avoid them. Whether at home in the Family Fountain Restaurant in Metamora, Illinois or at a roping in Arizona or Texas; I am not going to let someone spoil my confidence and optimism. It is a waste of time.

Focus on the positive; it will influence your behavior and the behavior of those around you. In every roping run, catch or miss, I try to find a major positive. I will also analyze the run for how I can improve the next time. I can always find a positive. Bobby Harris sets a fantastic example of optimism and confidence. He is inspiring to be around.

Flaming enthusiasm is another strong element in keeping a positive attitude. I enjoy every roping run, win or lose. Often if my partner misses, he or she will ride over and start to apologize. I just thank them for roping with me and explain that I enjoyed every second of the run.

Practice

Practice: To do repeatedly in order to become proficient

No matter what you are working to improve, practice is essential. It is often under-emphasized and under-utilized in developing a skill. Whether your field is management, customer service or sports, it takes practice to develop your talent, refine your skills and execute at the highest level.

Practice is seldom fun; more often, it is work. There are two great stories here that helped me accept the importance and value of practice.

Pete Rose was an outstanding hitter. "When Pete broke the record for the most base hits of anyone that ever played baseball everyone asked, 'How did you accomplish such an amazing feat'? 'Is it your hand-eye coordination?' 'No' was Pete's reply. 'Well it must be your ability to read a pitch or the fact that you have great speed.' To which Pete replied, 'It took me years to learn to read pitchers and as far as my speed, I am one of the slowest on the team. I think it might have something to do with the fact that I haven't missed batting practice in 19 years. Sometimes on days that batting practice wasn't required, I was the only guy to show up." Walt Woodard, *Super-Looper Magazine*, April 2001

I had the privilege of practicing with John Samsil, champion team roper, several winters in Wickenburg, Arizona. He passed some advice along one afternoon, as we were roping steers. His guidance describes the importance of quality practice: "Practice for competitive roping or to train your horse. Don't practice how to practice."

His statement about practicing for competition versus just practicing is profound. When you practice with John, there is no doubt that he walks the talk. He is very good, and it is not by accident.

Prayer

Prayer: a humble request to God

When it comes to prayer about my roping, I am very careful. I want to win the roping, but it is only a desire and not critical to my life. Usually I don't pray about it because I feel like I am primarily in it for fun and shouldn't be bothering the Lord with such trivial and frivolous issues. If it is a major event or closely tied to a goal, I do sometimes pray. In that situation I pray only that I will do my best and rope up to my potential. I will also pray that the competitors and the animals involved will be safe.

I will not wish my competitors bad luck. When I win a roping I want to win it because of my good performance, not because someone else failed to perform. I want to beat them at their best. If I can't beat them today, I will be back and try again tomorrow, next week, next month or next year.

Professional Help

Professional: Engaged in some sport or in an occupation for pay
Help: To make things better or easier

If you were really trying to get good at something, I mean really serious about it, why wouldn't you use professional help? You're thinking, of course, *I would*! Many people don't.

In 1994 I went to my first roping school. It was a three-day roping school taught by professionals Doyle Gellerman and Walt Woodard. They were the 1981 World Champion team ropers. It was a life-altering experience. I learned so much in so little time it was amazing. I went to schools the following two years with Doyle Gellerman and Bobby Harris. The learning continued at a phenomenal rate. From 1999 through 2003, I was fortunate to have Tanner Bryson, a top rodeo cowboy, help me. I went to his ranch two or three days during my three-month winter vacation in Arizona, and he would coach me. Here again, I learned a great deal.

In 2004 Bobby Harris invited me to his new one-week roping camp at his ranch in South Dakota. This was another pivotal experience in my roping progress. Bobby is a former world champion roper and skilled in all timed rodeo events. He is an outstanding coach and an extremely positive person.

His camp will take you to a whole new achievement level. I have attended for the last four summers and each year has been a significant growth experience. Plus, it is just plain fun.

I will confess to having difficulty realizing the importance of getting professional help. A prime example comes from my work experience. After 28 or 29 years at Caterpillar it was common in my managerial role to give some form of verbal presentation almost every day. You can imagine my surprise when Bill Cronk, one of my Division Managers, suggested I go to a seminar on public speaking. Bill had been trying to get me to join Toastmasters for some time. Finally I agreed, spent my three days in Chicago and found it interesting and helpful, but I really didn't think I had learned all that much. (Of course, no data on this issue.) A few days after I returned home, I had to give a presentation to the top 150 people in our Technical Services Division. I worked hard on that twenty-minute speech, doing my best to employ everything I had recently learned. After the meeting Ernie Blood came up to me, someone I had worked with for twenty-seven years, and said, "That was the best speech I ever heard Monte Alkire give." I sure appreciated his comment and still recall it twelve years later. That is a prime example of what professional help can do, even when you think you already know it all.

Imagine the improvement you could make with professional help. A true professional can help in many ways. They see things we don't see and know how to correct the problems. It is amazing.

If you're a golfer, tennis player, sales person, engineer or bowler, just contemplate three days or a week with your favorite professional coaching you. I highly recommend professional help.

See

Definition: To get knowledge of through the eyes

Whatever our focus or commitment is, we must learn to see the things going on around us that affect the outcome. Too often we become so involved or engrossed in the spirit of the moment, the grandeur of the event, the important people present, the audience, and/or the fanfare that we fail to see factors that are likely to affect the result.

We must train ourselves to cut through the atmosphere and see what is important. In sports as in business, there are critical variables that affect outcomes. In roping, we have typically six to nine seconds for our runs. We must learn to see and internalize many things to help us in the future. Perhaps you think you can already see really well. Spend some time with a professional in your activity and observe what they can see. You will be amazed. Understand the critical variables in your endeavor and make sure you see what is happening.

Slumps

Slump: A period of poor or substandard performance

Slumps will occur in our journey to excellence. We must stay positive and work through them. The key is to realize slumps will occur, and when they do, to deal with them in a professional manner. They can be brought on by a host of outside events or occurrences and often by the results of your team-mates. One of my worst slumps was a string of 8 weeks of steady competition and no paychecks. I asked a young cowboy friend of mine, Will Ward, what to do about slumps. His reply was, "Make 'em short," more cowboy logic.

I think Will's advice was simple and yet profound, but how could I "make 'em short?" I figured out what was wrong by examining the basics and mechanics of roping. I got professional help and tried different approaches and techniques. I continued to change things until my roping started to click again. I practiced until the problem was fixed, then set a new standard of excellence. Often, what you learn working out of a slump will take you to a new level of achievement.

Slumps will give you a gut check on your passion. When you're in doubt about whether all this work is worthwhile just ask yourself, "Am I having fun? Is this what I really enjoy? Will I go the extra mile? Am I willing to do whatever is required for as long as it takes to get through this? Will I work, problem solve, train and practice until I know I am ready again?"

With positive answers to the previous questions, you can tell yourself, "I knew slumps would occur. I know it will take work, time and perhaps some help to get through this. I am not afraid to risk failure before I succeed. This is what I love to do!" This approach will help you break your slump.

It may take hours, days, weeks or months. There is no magic solution or answer. Apply everything you have learned, seek outside help if necessary, and have faith in yourself and those around you.

Target and Aim

Target: An object to be aimed at in shooting
Aim: To sight a weapon at a target

The whole concept here is to be certain what you are aiming for, be precise in your aim, and don't be distracted by those things around the target or nearby. The more I thought about this, the clearer I could see its applicability in my sport. When I am roping I don't aim for the steer's head. I aim for the base of the left horn. I believe it is the same in many situations. Oral presentations are a good example. You present for 30 minutes, but what are you really trying to achieve?

If you aim precisely, chances are you won't miss by much.

Tough Spots

Tough Spot: Difficult or dangerous or uncomfortable situation

Maybe your biggest critic is in an audience and must sign off on a proposal you're making. Maybe it starts to rain at the roping or darkness is closing in. Perhaps you've drawn the toughest steer or worst bronc. Do your best and accept the result. "Sometimes you get in a tough spot, make a tough draw. When you do all you can do, that's all you can do!" — Ty Murray, Wrangler National Finals Rodeo Commentary

If you are unsuccessful, shake it off and get ready for your next chance. A success in these situations is inspiring, confidence building, and another step on the ladder of excellence.

Trying Hard

You have to figure out how to try as hard as you can without trying too hard. For me the best therapy for not trying too hard is to review mentally how hard I have practiced and how well I have prepared. With this background I know that all I have to do is go out and let it happen, nod for the steer and react. This works best for me. However, each athlete has to work through "trying hard" in his or her own mind. Every athlete has a different way of dealing with it. The best book I have ever read on this subject is *The Inner Game of Tennis* by W. Timothy Gallwey. Another excellent reference is *Mental Toughness Training For Sports: Achieving Athletic Excellence*, by James E. Loehr, Ed.D. Mr. Loehr will help you evaluate your performance and train yourself to improve.

Visualization

Visualization: To form a mental image

One way to overcome distractions is by employing visualization. It is a good way to upgrade your competitiveness. I find it extremely helpful to use visualization just before I make a run, and before I make my final preparations for the run.

"You can call it visualization or meditation, but when you think about something and you use your imagination and use detail, anything is possible. When I first started competing I would get to the arena and visualize my run. I would think about it in every little detail from the temperature to the smell. I could see my position going down the arena and I could see my rope hit its target. I would watch the rope come tight and the flag drop. I would do that over and over. I would run different patterns of the steer but always the same results: perfect.

"Through studies on human behavior they have concluded that the human mind can't tell the difference between reality and fiction. The example they used is when we dream. You know how scared you are and it's exactly the same way you would feel if it was really happening. Your mind can't tell the difference. You have to use detail in your visualizations to ingrain it into your mind." — Walt Woodard, *SuperLooper Magazine*, 2001

Here is a great story on this subject from professional football: "Joe Montana was being interviewed near the peak of his career. He was renowned for his passing ability. He had just thrown several outstanding passes. A reporter asked, 'Weren't you shocked when the receiver made that catch?' Joe said, 'No… not at all. I visualize every pass I throw being caught.'" As told by Dale Woodard, 1-13-04

The following is the most profound story on visualization I have ever heard:

"During the Vietnam War there was a fighter pilot that was shot down and captured. He was held against his will for two years in solitary confinement. The cage he was in was about seven feet tall and about seven feet wide. He was subjected to all kinds of terrible things, so to get through it he played golf everyday. Before he was shot down he had a four handicap. That means that when he played a round of golf, if par was 72 he would shoot 76. That is great golf for you non-golfers out there. You have to work long and hard and practice every chance you get to play at that level.

"So everyday when he woke up he would imagine he was at home, he would shower, get dressed and have a nice breakfast. He would drive to the golf course that he had played so many times near his home and he would hit a bucket of balls before he played. Once on the golf course, he would select each club with care and replace every divot after each shot. Once on the green he would repair his ball mark and someone else's to help keep the golf course pristine. Every detail was right down to the mark.

"It would take him about eight hours every day to play a round of golf from the time he left home until he returned. He said that his captors thought he was crazy because he would stand in his cell and with his hand, high over his head, swing the imaginary golf club and then watch his ball fly through the air.

"Finally came his freedom and when he returned home even though he was extremely malnourished he said that he wanted to play golf. They took him to his old golf course and he shot a 76.

"Everyone said that it was amazing that a man that had not played golf in more that two years could shoot four over par. To which he responded, 'On the contrary, I have practiced everyday for two years and I would have been very disappointed if I would have shot 80 because I have never practiced that much in all my life.' He had practiced in his mind and kept his skills sharp. It is amazing the power of our minds if only we can tap into that powerful source." — Walt Woodard, *SuperLooper Magazine*, 2002

I have read these stories several times and they energize me to do more with visualization. Visualization is a technique that I am presently under-utilizing. It is hard to discipline myself to take the time to practice by visualization. Many rainy days I could be practicing my roping in this fashion. I will get better at visualization!

Epilogue

On Friday February 3, 2007, I experienced my personal best during competitive roping. I entered a Ty Yost Roping in Surprise, Arizona. There were 610 teams of all ages competing for over $35,000 in prizes and trophy saddles.

The cattle were fast and strong. I rode my nine-year old horse, Paco. He was awesome! It was his first exposure to competing in a covered arena. Military fighter jets were constantly taking off and landing from the nearby Luke Air Force Base. The speaker system was close to the box and very loud. It was a huge test for the horse and he performed flawlessly.

Fortunately, I was really on my game; I rode well and roped as well as I ever have. It was a personal best. I didn't draw a check, but Herb Snow and I were in the top twenty teams. I know I have never roped better.

I also know it was a personal best in mental toughness. The day started with entering at 9:30 a.m. and roping 10 steers including the finals at 6:30 p.m. It was a major test for my horse and me, and we passed with flying colors. It really made for a great day.

How did I achieve this level of excellence? Through applying everything I have shared with you in this book plus all the technical and mechanical aspects of team roping.

I believe that much of what I have collected applies to many of our daily activities, whether it is job skills, interpersonal skills with family and friends, or recreational activities. If you start to use these approaches and references, you will personally be able to add significantly to what I have assembled here.

Whatever you do in life, *be sure to enjoy the journey*!

Team Roping References

American Cowboy Team Roping Association

Original Team Roping Association

Professional Rodeo Cowboys Association

Pro Rodeo Sports News

Spin To Win Rodeo Magazine

SuperLooper Magazine

Wrangler Team Roping Championships

United States Team Roping Championships

Recommended Reading

Mental Toughness Training For Sports:
Achieving Athletic Excellence
James E. Loehr, Ed.D.

The Inner Game of Tennis
 W. Timothy Gallwey

My Personal Best
John Wooten with Steve Jamison

And If You Play Golf, You're My Friend:
Further Reflections of a Grown Caddie
Harvey Penick with Bud Schrake

About The Author

Thirteen years ago I decided to learn to rope. I was in my mid-fifties; my wife and I found our nest empty. This translated to more discretionary time and recreational funds. A lifelong dream, learning to rope, suddenly became a reality. This period was also important as it began our pre-retirement era from my day job at Caterpillar Inc. As I entered this phase of life, I had no idea how much pleasure, learning, satisfaction and friendship I would derive from this whole undertaking. Roping has evolved into my passionate desire to become the best cowboy and horseman possible.

My work over the last 17 years of my career led me to really appreciate and understand the importance, difficulty and the value of constantly working to improve. During the 1980s, Caterpillar was in a fierce battle with Komatsu for dominance in the earthmoving market. We won! As a part of this struggle, I studied and implemented the best practices known for quality improvement, including the works of Dr. Joseph M. Juran, Dr. Edwards W. Deming, and Dr. Gayle W. McElrath. I attended seminars and workshops and talked with them at every opportunity. That experience, coupled with my inherent competitiveness, was a natural fit for enjoying continuous improvement and excelling in roping competition.

In 1997 I retired from Caterpillar Inc. after 33 years and started a new phase of my life. Then I really had time for my passion, roping. It was a natural thing for me to really study how to succeed, improve and excel.

Made in the USA